New Life Trails Devotion

Volume 1

Enduring Pain, Finding Purpose, Experiencing Peace

Deborah Renee Spears

10% of all proceeds will go to support the animals of New Life Trails. Visit newlifetrails.org.

Trilogy Christian Publishers

A Wholly Owned Subsidiary of Trinity Broadcasting Network

2442 Michelle Drive

Tustin, CA 92780

New Life Trails Devotion Volume 1: Enduring Pain, Finding Purpose, Experiencing Peace

For information, address Trilogy Christian Publishing

Rights Department, 2442 Michelle Drive, Tustin, Ca 92780.

For information about special discounts for bulk purchases, please contact Trilogy Christian Publishing.

Manufactured in the United States of America

10 9 8 7 6 5 4 3 2 1

Library of Congress Cataloging-in-Publication Data is available.

ISBN 979-8-88738-473-3

ISBN 979-8-88738-474-0 (ebook)

Dedication

Of the many experiences at New Life Trails, Logan's story is the most precious. Their family's story is the purest form of experiencing pain, understanding purpose, and establishing peace. Thank you for allowing us to be part of your story and sharing it with others.

Table of Contents

Preface

Having grown up on a farm and in poverty, I found tremendous solace from the animals on our family's farm. My love language with God has always been encapsulated in animals and nature, and I've passionately wanted to establish the opportunity for God to reach others through the same venue. As a special education teacher, I encounter so many who initially need to meet God at this level and in this place. Hence the establishment of New Life Trails. While I am CEO/Founder, my church and many others have partnered together to make this ministry a reality, but only through God's sovereign hand.

New Life Trails is a 501(c)(3) non-profit organization. It is located in Ponca City, Oklahoma. It resides on twenty-five acres of land and is home to fifty-two animals. Twenty of the animals are rescue animals. Our mission statement is, "*Partnering with animals to capture the hearts of individuals to provide intervention academically, emotionally, socially, and spiritually.*" We actively minister to children's homes, foster families, disabled and at-risk children, nursing homes, churches, schools and are available to hospice for children's intervention camps and home visits, as well as many other outreaches.

It was at a home visit that we met Logan and God began the ministry through Logan's Barn. Logan had terminal cancer. He had qualified for a trip to the San Diego Zoo through the Make a Wish Foundation. When he became sick too fast and could not go to the zoo, his family contacted New Life Trails and asked us to bring some animals to see him. We brought a newborn lamb to give to him, which was to be kept at the Trails for him for children to love. He named it Skittles. In addition, we brought a chicken, a rabbit, and a baby goat to see him. The chicken flew over and pooped on his cousin and caused Logan to laugh. The rabbit nestled up by his cheek so he could feel it because he was already paralyzed from the neck down from the cancer.

Logan told his dad and mom that we needed a red barn to keep the animals in. The Holy Spirit led me to share with Logan that someday New Life Trails would have a barn, and we would paint it red and call it Logan's Barn. *A teenage volunteer that went with me to take the animals to see Logan commented that she had never seen so much happiness and sadness in a room at the same time.* In only days, Logan went to be with Jesus. In lieu of flowers, the family asked for donations to build Logan's Barn. A year later the barn was built by volunteers and generous donators and dedicated to God's work.

Today, it houses any sick or small animal in bad weather. It is also a tutoring building for over fifty at-risk children. Hardly a day goes by that Logan's name is not mentioned and his story told to children with disabilities, community service workers, at-risk children, and many visitors. When any of the students or children complain about the difficulty of their lives, I take them to a wall that has Logan's story and pictures on it in the barn. There, I tell them that this little boy would give anything for one of your bad days. Although he had twenty surgeries before he was ten, he loved life. He would tell you today that life is a precious gift, and a minute must not be wasted.

Logan's family found a small place of peace in their hearts upon his passing because Logan's life would continue to have an additional purpose. Correspondingly, New Life Trails has a similar story for me. As I interact daily with community service individuals, students, and many visitors, I can connect with them because of the hardships of my life and the way, through Christ, *that my pain has led me to my purpose and peace.*

To learn more about New Life Trails and Logan's story, go to newlifetrails.org.

May God's love and His promises blanket your pain as the crystal white snow blanketed New Life Trails and Logan's Barn and covered all of its blemishes and inadequacies. May God reveal to you a *purpose* sharper than the cutting cold, and more endearing than the present pain.

Aware
DO all things without arguing and complaining,
that you may be blameless and harmless, the
sons of God"
D
Philippians 2:14
Available
With my soul have I DESIRED thee in
the nights yea with my spirit within me will
I seek thee early.
D
Isaiah 26:9a
Rely
Fear not, for I am with thee, be not DISMAYED
for I am God I will strengthen thee, yea I will
help thee, I will uphold thee with the right hand
of my righteousness
D
Isaiah 41:10

Introduction

Along a Trail, *On the Trail to Knowing God,* at New Life Trails there are wooden signs with three Bible verses written on each. They are consecutive from A to Z through a section of the Trail. They are preceded by a poem that was written to activate the verses in our hearts according to the Armor of God.

Aware, Available, Rely
If you want to know victory in your life,
you've got to know the scripture, Aware, Available, Rely.
Aware of what God expects from your life.
Available to Jesus to work and abide.
The next is the greatest, you've got to Rely.
Let's start with A and go to Z
and the next thing you know,
you're going to be free.
Now that you've got it in your heart,
it's not the end, it's just the start.

The *Aware* verses represent the Sword of the Spirit and the dividing that God's Word does between right and wrong. The *Available* verses represent the Breastplate of Righteousness and how God's righteousness shines through us the greatest when we apply these verses. The *Rely* verses represent the Shield of Faith, which are God's promises that we speak throughout the day as Satan attacks us with his lies.

Everyone wants to know *what their purpose is in life.* I believe that God does not always define the specific direction, but as we go, these principles are critical and envelop our purpose.

Over the years, I have put these verses to memory, and I can pray them throughout the day. The ABC's help me to categorize them and have key words in the verse that help me pull them up. Most of the time, I don't know what to pray. I just start with A and pray until I feel peace. Then I know the Holy Spirit has established that victory. I've always wondered what it meant spiritually *to Let Go and Let God.* I have heard it so many times but could not understand how to implement it. I believe it is through giving *thanks* that God's promises are validated in our lives. In Philippians we are told, "Do not be anxious about anything, but in every situation, by prayer and petition, with *thanksgiving*, present your requests to God. And the peace of God, which transcends all understanding, will guard your hearts and your minds in Christ Jesus" (Philippians 4:6,7 NIV).

Romans 4:17 tells us to "*call those things that are not as though they are.*" God says that without faith, it is impossible to please Him. As you say and pray these promises, if you do not feel they are real yet, keep claiming them until they are real in your life. I insert my children's names, my husband's, my church and, of course, New Life Trails into them. *I will start on my face before God and as I pray His promises, then I will rise until I am standing with my hands raised in the air to Him.* When you accepted Jesus as your Savior, you were filled with the Holy Spirit of God and you are complete in Him (Colossians 2:10). You must believe that you are: love when you have a right to hate, joy when you have a right to despair, peace when you have a right to be anxious, patient when you have a right to be impatient, kind when you have a right to be mean, gentle when you have a right to be harsh, self-controlled when you have a right to be self-willed, good when you have a right to be bad, and faithful when you have a right to be unfaithful.

When you can't see His hand, trust His heart.

I pray the animal stories will capture your heart as God intervenes spiritually into your life through the memorized Word of God.

Go to newlifetrails.org for printable copies of individual verses.

Cumulative Verses

A great general in history, Napoléon, said that the battle is won or lost fifteen minutes before it is fought. Do you have a plan to attack the fruit of the flesh, which is the opposite of the *Fruit of the Spirit* such as despair, anxiety, meanness, harshness, self-will, badness, and unfaithfulness? It is as important to know the enemy as it is to know your weapons, or you will be caught off guard and defeated. We must replace Satan's lies with God's truth.

Thank you, God, that "**A**" I can do ***ALL*** things through Christ who strengthens me (Philippians 4:13).

Thank you, God, that "**B**" I can ***BE*** confident that the work You began, You will complete until the day of Christ (Philippians 1:6).

Thank you, God, that "**C**" I am ***COMPLETE*** in Christ, the Head of all principalities and powers (Colossians 2:10).

Thank you, God, that "**D**" I do not need to fear, for You are with me, I do not need to be ***DISMAYED***, for You are my God, and You will strengthen me, yes, You will help me, yes, You will uphold me with the right hand of Your righteousness (Isaiah 41:10).

Thank you, God, that "**E**" There is no temptation that has taken me, but such is common to man, but God is faithful, who will not suffer me to be tempted above that which I am able but will with every temptation also make a way for me to ***ESCAPE***, that I may be able to bear it (1 Corinthians 10:13).

Thank you, God, that "**F**" You know the plans that You have for me, plans to prosper me and not harm me, plans to give me hope and a ***FUTURE*** (Jeremiah 29:11).

Thank you, God, that "**G**" I will ***GROW*** as I am faithful to desire and consume Your Word (1 Peter 2:2).

Thank you, God, that "**H**" You will restore health to unto me, and You will ***HEAL*** me of my wounds (Jeremiah 30:17).

Thank you, God, that "**I**" You will ***INSTRUCT*** me in the way that I should go, and You will guide me with Your eyes (Psalm 32:8).

Thank you, God, that "**J**" You will supply all my needs according to Your riches in Christ ***JESUS*** (Philippians 4:19).

Thank you, God, that "**K**" the peace of God which passes all understanding, will ***KEEP*** my heart and mind through Christ Jesus (Philippians 4:7).

Thank you, God, that "**L**" the ***LORD***'s hand is not shortened, that it cannot save me, neither is ear heavy, that it cannot hear (Isaiah 59:1).

Thank you, God, that **"M"** ***MANY*** are the afflictions of the righteous, but the Lord delivers me out of them all (Psalm 34:9).

Thank you, God, that **"N"** ***NOT*** by might, not by strength, but by My Spirit says the Lord (Zechariah 4:6).

Thank you, God, that "**O**" You have given unto me power to tread on serpents and scorpions, and ***OVER*** all the power of the enemy and nothing by any means shall hurt me (Luke 10:19).

Thank you, God, that "**P**" You will ***PERFECT*** that which concerns me (Psalm 138:8).

Thank you, God, that "**Q**" I am more than a ***CONQUEROR*** through Christ that loves me (Romans 8:37).

Thank you, God, that "**R**" I am the ***RIGHTEOUSNESS*** of God in Christ Jesus (2 Corinthians 5:21).

Thank you, God, that **"S"** ***Sin*** shall not have dominion over me, for I am not under the law, but under grace (Romans 6:14).

Thank you, God, that **"T"** You have led me as a captive in Your ***TRIUMPH*** and You use me to spread the aroma of the knowledge of You everywhere (2 Corinthians 2:14).

Thank you, God, that **"U"** to those who love God, all things work together ***UNTO*** good (Romans 8:28).

Thank you, God, that "**V**" I have this treasure in His earthen ***VESSEL*** that the excellency of the power is of God, and not me (2 Corinthians 4:7).

Thank you, God, that "**W**" when I pass through the ***WATERS***, You will be with me, and I go through the rivers, they will not overflow me, and when I walk through the fire, I shall not be burned, neither shall the flames kindle upon me (Isaiah 43:2).

Thank you, God, "**X**" that though I am troubled on every side, yet I am not distressed, ***PERPLEXED***, but not in despair; persecuted but not forsaken, cast down, but not destroyed; always bearing about in the body the dying of the Lord Jesus, that the life also of Jesus might be made manifest in my mortal flesh (2 Corinthians 4:7-10).

Thank you, God, "**Y**" that Your ***YOKE*** is easy, and Your burden is light (Matthew 11:28).

Thank you, God, "**Z**" that Jesus died for me so that I could live, but not for myself, but for Him (2 Corinthians 5:15).

As I pray these verses, I paraphrase them. It takes only a few minutes to pray these each morning, and you will be established with your shield of faith for the day.

DAY 1

A-Thank you God, that "I can do ***ALL*** things through Christ who strengthens me" (Philippians 4:13).

Resolved
(A Verse)

What lies are you believing from the enemy? Have you listened to your self-talk lately? What things are you saying or believing that you can't accomplish in your life today?

Having just finished her first horse ride by herself, she unmounted. Although I walked beside her while she rode, she repeatedly wanted to see my hands to verify that I was not touching the horse and that she was riding by herself. After the ride, she gleamed with pride as she went to get the tack box to groom her horse. I was helping her and brushing the opposite side of her horse. After she advised me that she didn't need any help, I looked around the side of the horse. She was attempting to lift her horse's foot to clean the hoof. My eyebrows raised instantly as I observed her ***resolve.*** I might add to my observation that she was just four years old, and Lightning is our biggest horse at the Trails. How could she be so confident and fervent in her abilities to handle this giant? Shaking my head, squinting my eyebrows, and tucking the side of my mouth into my cheek, I questioned. Then it came to me that she had never received within her spirit that she couldn't. She only believed that she could.

While, of course, there are many things that, in fact, I can't do. But how, when, and where did the list get extended to so many compartments of my life as a believer in a living God that says, "You can, in Me!" I catch myself saying too often: I can't love, I can't have joy, I can't have peace, I can't have patience, kindness, gentleness, self-control, and faithfulness. Who did I let speak these lies into my life and why did I receive them?

"I can do ALL things through Christ who strengthens me" (Philippians 4:13).

Dear Heavenly Father,

Help me today to have the ***resolve*** according to what You have told me in Your Word. Help me to live consistent with only that truth and to replace Satan's lies with Your truth.

Day 2

B-Thank you, God, that I can ***BE*** confident that the work that You have begun in my life, You will complete (Philippians 1:6).

Feathers
(B Verse)

Where do you turn for help when you face adversity? Are you deliberate in your plan or do you just face it as it comes? I've heard it said that he who has no plan, plans to fail. Have you identified the things that you are not going to turn to, as well as the things that you will turn to when you face trials and tribulations? The children of Israel spent forty years in the desert for a two-week trip because they never made a plan, or at least didn't follow it for when they faced tribulation.

In watching a mother hen and her four chicks yesterday, I was so blessed. When I came near to her pen, she fluffed up her feathers and gave a low-key call to her chicks to come into the shelter of her wings. She identified me as a danger and provided the protection that her chicks would need. Surprisingly, the chicks didn't go underneath of her, instead they went in between her feathers and nestled up to the warmth of her skin. This is such a beautiful picture of God's provision for His children. God's promises are there to complete the work that He began in us if we will find shelter in them. In the Bible, there are 5,467 promises. Each one is a feather of His love. There have been so many times when I have been afraid: for my children, my parents, my husband, my church, my finances, my abilities, my peace, my joy, and so forth. In my fear, God has led me to His faithfulness through His promises.

"I am confident that the work that God has begun, He will complete" (Philippians 1:6).

Dear Heavenly Father,

Help me to have a plan to turn to you when fear comes upon me. I know it is not a matter of *if* it comes, but when. Help me to identify the places that I am *not* going to turn to as well as the promises that I am going to turn to. I know it is important to know both.

Day 3

C-Thank you, God, that I am ***COMPLETE*** in You, the Head of all principalities and powers (Colossians 2:10).

Frozen
(C Verse)

Are you allowing sin to accumulate in your life? Is it because of the lack of knowledge of sin, or the lack of the knowledge of God?

Freezing harsh weather brings an ache that goes all the way through to my bones when I'm at the Trails. The mornings are filled with the trek from one water tank to the next. Breaking the ice so that the livestock may continue to thrive is critical. I do not like it, and it reminds me of sin as it wants to *freeze*, isolate, and shut me down.

As I was breaking ice on the animal's water yesterday, I found it interesting that there were different thicknesses in different water troughs. The bigger the water trough; the *thinner* the layer of ice that had accumulated. Conversely, the smaller the trough; the *thicker* the ice accumulation. As I was contemplating the difference, I thought of my own spiritual life. When I was a younger Christian and my knowledge and love for God were smaller, sin was so much more prevalent and stubborn in my life. I believed my spiritual strength came from within myself. However, the larger my love, knowledge, and relationship with God became, the thinner the accumulation of sin in difficult times. I knew that my strength came from my God within me and through thanking Him for His presence, power, and provision in my life. My *completeness* was in Him. When I align with God and examine my life daily and even multiple times daily, the sin (despair, anxiety, impatience, and so forth) does not accumulate through the day, the weeks, the months, and even the years.

I am *complete* in Christ the Head of all principalities and powers (Colossians 2:10).

Dear Heavenly Father,

Help me to examine myself continually. Help me to turn to You, know You, know Your Word, and Your power that meets my needs so that my trough is bigger and bigger in You. Help me to know when the brokenness of this world is creating a *frozen* layer of sin in my life because I am looking to myself, the world, and others for *completeness.*

DAY 4

D-Thank you, God, that I do not need to fear for You are with me, I do not need to be ***DISMAYED,*** for You are my God, and You will strengthen me, yes, You will help me; You will uphold me with the right hand of Your righteousness (Isaiah 41:10).

Potholes
(D Verse)

Have you ever encountered something in your life that knocked you off the path that you were on? Did you get back on the path? How long did it take you?

When I was a young girl, I used to ride my bike down a hill that merged into the long lane that led to our old wooden home. We lived in the depths of the country and the lane had deep grasping ruts and potholes in it from the vehicles' attempts to make it home. Riding their bikes after the rain, my brothers would attempt and successfully master the potholes and ruts each time they rambled the lane. They did not question their ability to make it; they had no fear and just did it. But me? That was a different story. Each time, the attempt left me with the bike toppled over on top of me or knocked off the course into the fence. I was *dismayed.* Eventually, I would make it and the feeling was of elation! I could just feel those handlebars surrendering to my tugs and pulls, and it was so worth the struggle. However, after the next rain, there would be new potholes and ruts. Somehow, once I decided there was no giving up, the potholes never seemed as intimidating as they once were.

As I have aged, I have found life to be much like those potholes and ruts in the lane. As difficult times have come in downpours, they have brought a plethora of potholes and ruts. I remember when New Life Trails first started. We were not established in the community, and we did not have financial support. When I went to the feed shed, all that we had was donated dog food. I petitioned God; however, I was willing to just feed dog food. Within the hour, a lady came by to visit the facility, and without saying anything to her, she donated the exact amount that we needed for feed. God has continued to work in miraculous ways to meet the needs of New Life Trails. Those moments have been visuals in front of me to establish my faith to master the crazy ruts and potholes of life that are grasping to throw me to the ground in a new way after each storm.

"Do not fear for I with you, do not need to be ***DISMAYED,*** for I am your God, I will strengthen you, yes, I will help you; I will uphold you with the right hand of my righteousness" (Isaiah 41:10).

Dear Heavenly Father,

I know that life will be tough. I live in a fallen world, and I am subject to its decline. I know Your desire is to use each pothole and rut to make me stronger and more confident in You. I know that I must intentionally remember Your provision to not be *dismayed* by the depths of the ruts and potholes in situations. Help me to feel the warmth of Your hand upon mine, and the strength of Your arm around my shoulder as I do not go around but through the things set before me.

DAY 5

E-Thank you, God, that there is a way to ***ESCAPE*** the expectations of the world and myself (1 Corinthians 10:13).

Backwards
(E Verse)

Do you ever feel that you are backwards in a world going forward? Do you use your backwardness as an excuse for dysfunction, or for an opportunity to embrace ministry in a unique way?

Partnering with the Trails, my youngest daughter shares her unique animals with us. When she brought us a few new chickens, I thought one of them was just having a really bad hair day. As I examined her closer, her feathers were truly backwards. She is a frizzle chicken, and her name is Johnie. She is pitch black and beautiful, but very different. After inspecting her, I couldn't help but ask myself why she was created with her feathers backwards. It just seemed wrong. However, just the question gave me the answer. When I gaze over the chickens in our henhouse, it is a quick and routine glance. They are all pretty much standard and doing the standard thing that chickens—do until I get to Johnie. Then, I stop observe, examine, question, and even reflect on her presence and purpose in the flock. With each of our animals at the Trails, we desire that one more part of the personality of God is brought to light, honored, and adored. Uniqueness is a quality to be embraced in ourselves and certainly in our God.

When I ask why Johnie's breed was made with feathers backwards, it also leads me to the question of why God allows physical disabilities, sickness, mental and emotional disorders, poverty, abuse, pain, and rejection. To embrace the answer to such a question, I must step back from the hole in the fence that I am looking through and see the whole picture of God's plan. God created a perfect world to share and experience with us. Our nature allowed sin to enter the world and with sin came all the imperfections. Then, He sent His Son to provide a way for us to, once again, be in perfection with Him in eternity. The purpose of our time here on earth is not to establish or live in perfection, but to use absolutely everything within our grasp to give the opportunity for individuals to stop and examine where they are spiritually and what is God's call upon their lives.

When I am tempted to become a victim of my circumstances, it's because I compare myself and my abilities to seemingly perfectness in the world. I just seem wrong, like Johnie's backward feathers. However, *God provides a way of escape* from this temptation. In that, my uniqueness is a way to get individuals to stop, look, and listen to the purpose of their own unique circumstances in their life and how God calls them to eternal salvation and abundant life in Him.

"There hath no temptation taken you, but such is common to man, but God who is faithful, who will not suffer you to be tempted above that which you are able, but will with the temptation, also make a way for you to ***escape***, that you may be able to bear it" (1 Corinthians 10:13).

Dear Heavenly Father,

Help me to embrace the things that are different, even backwards, about myself and my circumstances to the world. Help me to use them to get others to stop, look, and ask why I am okay when everything seems so wrong. Help me be able to share that I have a purpose for my pain and because of that, I have peace.

Day 6

F-Thank you God, that You know the plans that You have ***FOR*** me. They are plans for good and not for evil, to give me a future and a hope (Jeremiah 29:11).

Frightened
(F Verse)

What fear is so great in your life that you can hardly move forward? How can you get past that fear?

Having three newborn lambs, Missy is guaranteed a stable at New Life Trails. She only has two teats and with three lambs, that can be a problem. In addition, she has been pulled from her herd, which is her support system and has a big black Angus cow in the pen beside her. She was never gentled in the herd, so she wants nothing to do with human contact! In Missy's eyes, life seems unbearable, but there are things that she doesn't know! There is a plan in place! We have her penned: to keep her babies safe from coyotes, to give her extra feed and hay, to have fresh water, to make sure she has enough milk, to supplement the lambs if they have need, and to gentle her and the lambs to be able to supplement their diet. Our plans for her are for good, not for evil, to give her and her lambs hope and a future.

As I saw the panicked look on this sweet ewe's face, I had to ask myself if I have ever felt like this ewe looks. Have I ever felt overwhelmed and unsure? Lately, it seems like difficult circumstances won't let up. Unimaginable things are happening. I find myself shaking my head and wondering what is going on. For me to go forward, I must surrender to the plan in place and trust. If God gave His Son for me to have eternal life, then He will care *for* the life He has given me while I am here on this earth.

"For I know the plans I have for you, declares the Lord. They are plans for good and not for evil, to give you a future and a hope" (Jeremiah 29:11).

Dear Heavenly Father,

As one thing after another seems to be happening wrong, and I can't see why, help me with confidence to know that these events were not meant to destroy me, but to make me stronger. Help me to trust and find strength that what I am going through will help and enable me for the journey ahead, just like with Missy, the ewe.

DAY 7

G-Thank you, God, that I will ***GROW*** as I am faithful to desire and consume Your Word (1 Peter 2:2).

Established
(G Verse)

How do you plan to grow spiritually? Do you have a plan? Will you make a plan?

Having been without the initial lifesaving colostrum, a baby calf was brought to New Life Trails. The calf's tongue had not been strong enough to grasp the teat of the cow after birth. By the time the calf and cow had been identified as needing help, the calf was already in critical danger. While it's not proven, many ranchers believe that this danger will follow them through life; they can just die at any time. Without this established source of antibodies, there is always the risk of not living. Despite knowing that calf might not make it, we fell in love with her automatically and she was given the name "Little Bit."

Correlating to the Christian walk, the Bible talks about the importance of the milk of the Word in our journey. Understanding and knowing who I am in Christ upon salvation is everything and is connected so intimately with the promises of God. How can I fight against the darkness of the world and its messages to me without knowing who I am spiritually? Knowing the promises of God is truly the colostrum with its antibodies to establish me as a believer. Once I am established in who I am, what my purpose is, where to find answers, and how to apply these principles to my life, then I can face all the hardships in life with victory. Without this foundation, I could die on the journey at any point.

"As newborn babies desire the sincere milk of the Word that you may *grow* thereby" (1 Peter 2:2).

Dear Heavenly Father,

Help me to make the time to know and memorize Your promises in Your Word that I may be established in who I am in You. Also, help me to be mindful and intentional when someone is saved to make available to them Your promises of who they are in You, so they will have a firm foundation in You to fight off all the spiritual diseases of this world.

Day 8

H- Thank you, God, that You will restore ***HEALTH*** unto me, and You will heal me of my wounds (Jeremiah 30:17).

Packed
(H Verse)

What trips you up in life spiritually? How will you recover from being tripped up? Do you have a recovery plan?

Tripping over air is one of my qualifying characteristics! However, this time it was a tree root that I tripped over. I guess I was thinking that I would keep myself from falling when I reached out and grabbed a tree. Instead of stopping the fall, the tree's bark skinned my inner arm while leaving a one- centimeter square piece of bark in my arm. After a mini surgery, the doctor told me to keep it packed until the wound healed from the inside to the outside. It was so gross poking a strip of medicine into a hole in my arm! In addition to packing it, it was important to keep the wound open so that the skin wouldn't heal over and cause even deeper infection. As I observed the hole previous to its packing, it disturbed my heart as I looked at its depth.

Corresponding to the visual of the hole in my arm, I know that my spiritual heart has holes in it that need to be healed. Life has tripped me up with many things such as neglect, abuse, rejection, failure, divorce, death, financial ruin, and so forth. All of the above and many more holes have needed to be *packed*. The questions I have faced are, will I keep them open to true healing, and what will I pack them with? The world has its prescriptions for *packing*, and it's called addictions. Addictions have an appearance of being a healing agent. However, they only close the opening of the wounds with their temporary anesthesia and no healing transpires. Thankfully, there is the One that came that we might have life and have it more abundantly (John 10:10). He calls us to *pack* our wounds with the living, healing Word of God; His promises through thanksgiving.

A-thank You, God, that I can do *ALL* things through Christ who strengthens me (Philippians 4:13). (I can write my own story in Christ instead of allowing others to write it for me.)

B-thank You, God, that I can be confident that the work You *BEGAN* in me, You will complete (Philippians 1:6). (This is not the end! The tools of what I have been through do not define me; they equip me!)

"I will restore *HEALTH* unto you, and I will heal you of your wounds" (Jeremiah 30:17).

My Dear Heavenly Father,

Help me to recognize the world's counterfeits that are a facade for healing. Help me when the world has left a hole in my spirit to *pack* it with Your healing Word until it truly heals from the inside out.

Day 9

I-Thank you, God, that You will ***INSTRUCT*** me in the way that I should go, and You will guide me with Your eyes (Psalm 32:8).

Naughty Spot
(I Verse)

Have you identified your spiritual naughty spot? What plans do you have in place to detour it?

When riding Lightning, our largest quarter horse at New Life Trails, he is very willing to comply with my son's request to directions until we get close to the barn where he is fed and saddled. Then, he rambunctiously pulls the reins and tries to head to the barn every time! If my son waits until he reaches that *"naughty spot,"* then it's too late to recover. However, if my son plans ahead of time and starts directing him away and giving him inspiring kicks to walk on through the spot, he is so much more successful!

Similarly, if we spiritually, emotionally, and even physically know our naughty spots, then we can be so much more successful in being victorious over our weaknesses. For instance, when I get gas in my car, I used to go inside and pay for it, get a soda, and a candy bar. When I started eating healthier, I would tell myself that I couldn't do that but went inside the store to pay, where I always gave in anyway. Now when I pull into the gas station, I tell myself ahead of time that I am going to pay for my gas with the debit card outside and not go in. It works!

That is just one of a thousand examples of where the Spirit is willing, but the flesh is weak. Sometimes, I struggle with relationships, the things I watch, how long I watch them, the things I listen to, friends that I follow into trouble, and so forth. Daniel 1:8 says that Daniel purposed ahead of time not to defile himself with the king's food and wine. The key part of that verse for me was that he purposed ahead of time. God promises that He will instruct us through His Holy Spirit, but we need to be available for Him to do His work by taking time to reflect, plan, seek Godly counsel, listen, and watch things that the Spirit can work through, and partner with those that have the same heart in Christ.

Thank you, God, that You will *instruct* me in the way that I should go, and You will guide me with Your eyes (Psalm 32:8).

Dear Heavenly Father,

Help me take the time to identify my weak areas. Once identified, help me to have a plan to be victorious over my naughty spots in Your strength.

DAY 10

J-Thank you, God, that You will supply all my needs according to Your riches in Christ ***JESUS*** (Philippians 4:19).

Holding Down
(J Verse)

Do you have trouble trusting God? Do you fight His will and direction for your life when it isn't consistent with your plan?

There are so many things that we experience because we live in a fallen world. We, as human beings, brought sin into this world by our disobedience, and humanity will suffer until we are in our eternal home with God. God created a perfect world for us, and then he established a perfect home for us to live in forever. In addition, He gave His Son to pay the price for our sin so that He could be with us through the valleys and into our eternal home. God is not the bad guy. Can you trust Him to equip and sustain you through the turbulence of life?

Recently, our little milking goat, Sunflower, has been refusing to be milked. When I am guiding her into her milking position, she will dig her feet into the ground and will not be moved. If you have ever tried to pull a goat somewhere it doesn't want to be, you know what I mean when I say that she would not be moved! Of course, she is bleating with cries that equate to "WHY?" After the back-and-forth struggle, I give my most fervent jerk, and capture her under my arm in a position to *HOLD* and milk her.

This is her purpose, and she must succumb to it. We use her milk to nourish and strengthen Athena, the Trails' guardian dog.

I know she doesn't like giving her milk to a dog. It must irritate her to see Athena lying there waiting and to hear Athena's slobbery laps of her precious milk. What Sunflower doesn't understand is that Athena may one day save her life from a predator. We know of danger, destruction, and despair that Sunflower cannot know, comprehend, or understand. Only a couple of months ago, one of our other animals was attacked and killed by a wild dog. That is why Athena came to us at the Trails. For Sunflower, we simply need her to trust us for what is best.

Wow! Trust is such a difficult word to write about, especially when it reflects on my own life. I have hated the valleys that God placed before me. During those valleys, I'm sure I looked like Sunflower digging my feet into the ground and pulling back while crying "WHY?" All the time, God was *holding* me down to fulfill the purpose that I had asked Him to complete in my life. Even recently, God took me from the Trails for two years and put me into a virtual training program. Many days, I cried, "Why God?" I even felt like I was being punished. However, now God has brought me back to the Trails and there is so much clarity as each day brings a new revelation of the tools that God has given me to fulfill His purpose for my life.

"My God will supply all your needs according to His riches in glory by Christ Jesus" (Philippians 4:19).

Dear Heavenly Father,

Help me to trust you. When I can't see Your hand, help me to trust Your heart.

DAY 11

K-Thank you, God, that Your peace that passes all understanding will ***KEEP*** my heart and mind through Christ Jesus (Philippians 4:7, KJV).

Cocklebours
(K Verse)

Have you ever had something difficult get ahold of you, emotionally or spiritually? Did it get so entangled in your being that it seemed impossible to remove? Bitterness is a burr that has many points and the longer it remains, the more entangled it becomes.

Irritatingly, every year when the cockleburs die and get ready to seed, they hang loosely to the plant. Anything that rubs against them, they attach to with their prickly points. The closer to the ground, the more vulnerable to them an animal is at the Trails. Of all the animals, our pot belly pigs maneuver closest to the ground. While their body hair doesn't lend itself to these nasty cockleburs, their tails do. Even if I remove most of the plants from their pen, they still find the ones that are hidden behind a tree stump or somewhere that I have missed. In only a matter of days, the ends of their tails are a matted, prickly mess that will rub sores against their skin. Removing those monsters is a task for only the brave at heart. However, once they are gone, there is one happy pig!

How like our fleshly nature and sin this scenario mimics! As I go through a day, a week, a month, or even a year. I pick up bad habits, bitterness, despair, anxiety, self-will, unfaithfulness, and so forth. I may even have thought that I cleaned the area in my life of situations where I could pick up things, but somehow at a point of reflection; I see I have a tangled mess. In God's amazing love, compassion, and mercy, He *keeps* my heart and mind as He works in my life to remove everything that is not consistent with who I am in Him. Yes, it is painful as some have embedded themselves deeply, but I know that I cannot go forward with my purpose in Christ while allowing these things to be attached to my being.

"And the peace of God, which passeth all understanding, shall keep your hearts and minds through Christ Jesus" (Philippians 4:7, KJV).

Dear Heavenly Father,

Help me to reflect daily on the condition of my heart and spirit in You, so that I don't have lingering things in my life that will prick and torment me. Help me to rest in your peace as You work in my life to perfect the one that You love.

DAY 12

L-Thank you, God, that the ***Lord's*** hand is not shortened that it cannot save me, neither His ear heavy that it cannot hear (Isaiah 59:1).

Plugged In
(L Verse)

What do you plug into for the emotional and spiritual power that is needed to make it each day? Is it something that could lead to an addiction?

While it is critical to memorize scripture to know who, what, where, when, and how. If we do not know, understand, and believe in the power that provides the ability to activate these principles, then we are still going to fall short of the victory that God has for us. We must know our God! We must know His names and who He is and the work that He does in His people. Without this knowledge, we are relying on our own strength and power. It's like vacuuming with a vacuum that isn't *plugged in.*

There is an outlet outside the office at New Life Trails that we often access as a source of power. It provides the power to so many works at the Trails. Running electricity to heat water, charging power tools, providing heat lights at night for baby animals, and so forth. However, even though the power is there, it would not benefit the Trails if we did not know and believe the power was there and access it! When the disciples and Jesus were in the boat in the storm, they feared for their lives. They addressed Jesus as Teacher, not as Lord, Savior, Provider, or Rescuer. They may have known the scriptures and principles that Jesus had taught them, but they still did not know the power within Him. In Hosea 4:6, God says, "My people are destroyed for lack of knowledge."

In accordance, the Lord's prayer starts with *Our Father who art in heaven, hallowed be Thy name*. When Jesus was teaching us how to pray, the first emphasis was on God's names, who He is, and the power that comes with His presence. When I go through the storms of life of sickness, poverty, isolation, emptiness, rejection, or betrayal and do not "*plug in*" to God as Savior, Healer, Shepherd, Friend, Provider, Rescuer, and so forth, then I am resigning to the hopelessness of depending on my powers and abilities.

"Behold, the LORD'S hand is not shortened, that it cannot save; neither his ear heavy, that it cannot hear" (Isaiah 59:1, KJV).

Heavenly Father,

Help me to make the time to learn and know Your names and know who You are, so I will "*plug in*" to You as I face life each day.

Day 13

M-Thank you, God, that ***MANY*** are my afflictions, but
You deliver me out of them all (Psalm 34:19).

Chasing Chickens in the Rain
(M Verse)

What is your reaction when things go awry? Are you angry or hopeless? What do you do with those feelings? Are the emotions wrong? Or is it just what we do with the emotions that is right or wrong?

A character trait from New Life Trails is self-control. It is to stop, pray, and do what's right. We submit to God, resist the Devil and He will flee from you (James 4:7). I consider our emotions to be the basic training ground for the Christian walk. Without the wrong choice, we couldn't be trained to make the right choice. So, God allows opportunities to come our way many times during the day. He is hoping that at some point we get it!

When we have a right to hate, we love,
When we have a right to despair, we have joy.
When we have a right to have anxiety, we have peace,
When we have a right to be impatient, we are patient
When we have a right to be mean, we are kind
When we have a right to be harsh, we are gentle
When we have a right to be bad, we are good
When we have a right to self-will, we use self-control
When we have a right to be unfaithful, we are faithful

With many visitors frequenting the Trails, we are bound to have mishaps at some point. The chicken pen seems to be the center of the mishaps because when the chicken door is opened, there is always a hesitation upon entering. I think it has something to do with roosters and flogging. Recently, over half of the chickens were out, and it was starting to rain. As we began to chase the chickens, the sprinkles turned into a downpour. The chickens and everyone chasing the chickens were dripping wet. The only thing harder than catching a chicken is catching a wet chicken in slippery mud. All of the sudden, laughter filled the paddock as one after the other slipped in the mud and fell. I've heard it said that if you don't laugh, you will be crying. It is a choice that we make over and over again whether or not to act in the flesh or in the Spirit of God when we face those difficult situations.

"Many are the afflictions of the righteous, but the Lord delivers him out of them all" (Psalm 34:19, KJV).

Dear Heavenly Father,

Help me to choose to be who I am in You. Help me to replace negative thoughts with songs and scriptures of victory.

DAY 14

N-Thank you, God, that Your work in me is ***NOT*** done by might, not by power, but by Your Spirit (Zechariah 4:6).

Reaching the Cross
(N Verse)

Can you be saved on your own merits? Can you live a victorious life in Christ on your own merits?

Enveloping us with its heat, summer was here in its full force. To display the beauty of God's creation, we planted flower beds along the Trails. When it's spring with a lot of rain, that is a wonderful idea. However, when summer and its heat arrive, it becomes an arduous task to keep them watered. Stepping out of my comfort zone, I decided to engineer a watering system with water hoses that had been donated. I had wrestled with it for a week, and I was so frustrated that I could not get to the end where the biggest flower bed was by the cross. *I just couldn't make it to the cross...* Thankfully, a former architect who volunteers at the Trails to keep the animals and vegetation watered noticed my struggle. In a fraction of my time, he had the whole system set up right to the base of the Cross.

I couldn't help but think how similar this situation was to man's effort to get spiritually to the cross. We try good works, church attendance, being a good person, and many other useless techniques that leave us coming up short. *We just can't get to the cross.* Jesus said, "I am the way, the truth, and the life, no one comes to the Father, except through me" (John 14:6) and He says in John 6:44, "No one can come to me unless the Father who sent me draws them."

"*Not* by might, *not* by power, but by My Spirit" (Zechariah 4:6).

Dear Father God,

Help me to continually be aware of the struggles of those You bring into my world. Help me be willing to take the time to introduce them to you and walk with them to *truly reach the cross* where our salvation and abundant life was paid for.

DAY 15

O-Thank you, God, that You have given me power to tread on serpents and scorpions, and ***OVER*** all the power of the enemy and nothing shall by any means hurt me (Luke 10:19).

Earthquaked
(O Verse)

Have you ever heard the phrase, "Let go and let God"? How does a person let go of their cares and concerns that are so deeply intertwined with their heart and mind?

Last week, we had an earthquake that registered 4.5. As we read Facebook posts, everyone processed and handled the experience differently. Some dealt with things being broken or displaced and were scared, while others were in disbelief. At the Trails, one of our very pregnant goats lost her balance and toppled upside down. The weight that she was carrying made her lose her balance in the quake.

In the same way, many times I am carrying so much weight emotionally and even spiritually that when my world quakes from things such as sickness, death, disappointment, and anxiety, I go down into despair and I'm sure that I look just like our momma goat with her feet sticking up in the air. God did not create me to carry so much. That is why Jesus came and instructed us to cast our cares upon Him.

“Behold, I give unto you power to tread on serpents and scorpions, and *over* all the power of the enemy: and nothing shall by any means hurt you” (Luke 10:19, KJV).

Dear Heavenly Father,

Help me be aware of situations that I’m carrying, of which I should know better. Help me be willing to lay those things at your feet and trust You, so that I have the strength to face each day’s quakes and stay on my feet.

Day 16

P- Thank you, God, that You will ***PERFECT*** that which concerns me (Psalm 138:8).

Blooming in the Fence
(P Verse)

What spiritual challenges do you find in your world daily? How will you make yourself available to God to perfect His work in your life?

I love my flowers that are in my flowerbed that are defined by a beautiful border of rocks. They have an existence of being nurtured that includes watering, fertilizing, and weed pulling. However, there is something uniquely beautiful and alluring about a flower that has survived in the wild. While feeding one of our animals, I caught a glimpse from the corner of my eye of a beautiful sunflower alone in the fence line. It had survived the lawnmower, the tractor, the horses' feet, human hands, the weather, and pesticides. Its beauty was not only in its colors, but its survival. So beautifully, God alone was its sustenance.

I couldn't help but think about the similarities between the flower and the Christian that is ministering outside the walls of the church. Many times, the Holy Spirit is the sole source of strength. The depth of intimacy with God glistens from their presence. I love to go to my church and fellowship, encourage, plan evangelism, and learn of God, which is called for in His Word. He instructs us to not forsake the assembling of ourselves together, that we can encourage one another that when we are tempted, we can stand.

However, as the church, we are often only identified within the borders of the building. It is so beautiful to observe a believer that is practicing their faith outside those borders. Outside in the world, where they have survived the anxiety, despair, hate, meanness, harshness, unfaithfulness, badness, self-will. Amazingly, God perfects the believers that are salt and light out in the world of fence lines and within the borders of the church building.

"The LORD will *perfect* that which concerneth me" (Psalm 138:8, KJV).

Dear Jesus,

Help me to not only bloom within the physical borders of my church, but in the fence lines of the world where I can draw others to You in eternal and abundant life. Help me to desire the intimacy that comes from sensing Your presence and Your Power ministering to another.

DAY 17

Q-Thank you, God, that I am more than a ***CONQUER-OR*** through Christ that loves me (Romans 8:37).

Rescued
(Q Verse)

Do you think that you must do everything to be victorious in a situation? Can you see that helping someone else can be victorious, too?

While we have many rescued animals at New Life Trails, last week was our first time to rescue animals to be relocated somewhere other than New Life Trails. We just weren't set up for the needs of these animals. At first, it was a very frustrating feeling to not have the resources needed to help them, but we were soon to discover that there was great delight in connecting them with someone who does. This was a note we received from one of the homes that took one of the animals that was a desperately crippled donkey with long hooves that twisted as they came out, *"He is so gentle! My son is spoiling him like crazy lol. He put a lead rope and halter on him and he didn't throw one fit about it. Thank you for telling me about him. I think everyone here is as happy that he is here as he is. He is fitting in great! Thank you for bringing him into our lives."* My heart was so blessed that my eyes were filled with tears. When mountains need moved, God sometimes gives us a shovel, and sometimes he wants us to pass the shovel to someone else so they may share in the blessing of being part of a great work.

This is so much the story of New Life Trails. When God put the vision of the ministry in my heart, I was going to write a book and sell it to make the money to run the ministry. It had been ten years and God had not allowed me to publish one book. Instead, He asked me to open the needs of New Life Trails to my church and my community. In God establishing the care of the Trails this way, hundreds of people are part of its story and are a critical part of every salvation, every discipleship, every hug, every smile, and every burden lifted and shared. Truly, God's ways are higher than our own (Isaiah 55:9).

"In all these things we are more than *conquerors* through him who loved us" (Romans 8:37).

Dear Heavenly Father,

Help me to know when you are calling me to a task and when you are calling me to hand a task to someone else?

Day 18

R-Thank you, God, that I am the ***RIGHTEOUSNESS*** of God in Christ Jesus (2 Corinthians 5:21).

Hidden
(R Verse)

Are things always as they appear?

We have a coal black mini horse at the Trails; her name is Silver. When we share with visitors what her name is, they look at us in confusion. When Silver was born, she was the softest, fluffiest, most delicate light shade of gray. Her appearance was breathtaking. As magnificent as her color was, her spirit was even greater. She was gentle, affectionate, and yielding. God has used her to melt many hearts and to express His love and presence in a visual representation.

However, as she grew, the downy gray fell away it to reveal the beautiful, dark, deep black which had previously been *hidden*. In spite of her color change when I behold her, I see that newborn ball of fluff. In Romans 4:17, God calls things that are not as though they are. He is referring to Abraham's seed being established, even though he was old and his wife was past childbearing. Seeing things that are not as though they are, a principle all through the Bible, and a foundational part of our salvation today. We are perfect, sinless, complete, the righteousness of God as a Christian, yet we appear to not be. There are two parts to our being once we become a Christian, the new creation and the shadow. The shadow is not who we are, but it is there until the day we are with our Savior in Heaven.

Silver is very much the spirit and heart of that ball of fluff when I look at her through my eyes, yet she is not when the world looks at her. 2 Corinthians 5:17 tells us that anyone that is in Christ is a new creation and that the old things have passed away and behold all things are new. This is who we are in Christ; a presence that God created at the moment of salvation. As we trek through this journey of life, we are to use who we are in Christ as a plumb line. We continually identify and realign our actions until we are with our Savior. As we carry a shadow of the old nature that attempts to cast its presence over who we are in Christ.

"God made Him who had no sin to be sin for us, so that in Him we might become the *righteousness* of God" (2 Corinthians 5:21).

Dear Heavenly Father,

Help me to be continually mindful of who I am in You, and the tremendous price that Jesus paid for me to have the new life of love when I have a right to hate, joy when I have a right to despair, peace when I have a right to be anxious, patient when I have a right to be impatient, kind when I have a right to be mean, gentle when have a right to be harsh, good when I have a right to be bad, and faithful when I have a right to unfaithful.

Day 19

S-Thank you, God, that ***SIN*** shall not have dominion over me, for I am not under the law, but under grace (Romans 6:14).

Failed?
(S Verse)

When do I resign to failure? How far do I go? How long do I keep trying? When do I call it quits? There are things that we should walk away from at different points, but not in our spiritual endeavors to align to who we are in Christ. It is a lifelong journey, and we only fail when we stop trying.

Raining relentlessly, the ground was saturated as I trekked through the pasture to check on a mare that was close to foaling. My eyes were filled with delight as I saw her fragile body standing next to her mother, and her markings were a spotted blaze. White dots looked like raindrops on her blaze. How appropriate that she was born in the rain, and so her name would be Rain as well. In the days to come, we would love, play, and acclimate her to the world of New Life Trails and its ministries. Rain flourished as she grew and seemed to fit into her role at the Trails so beautifully. However, when it came time to take her to the next level, she was not able to adjust. We attempted trainer after trainer, and the news would be consistently the same. "She will never be able to be used at the Trails because she will not give up her buck." One trainer even told us that she should be sold to a rodeo as a bronco. We could not even bear to hear such proclamations. There had to be a way. We just had to find that way.

Consistent with the struggles of Rain, I fight my old nature day in and day out. While Rain fights her nature to buck when a saddle is put on her, I fight a multitude of demons from overeating, drinking soda, watching too much TV and habits that would make an endless list. While 2 Corinthians 5:17 tells us that we are new creations in Christ, we know that Paul tells us in Romans how we are and will continue to fight against the flesh. In my circle, and with our precious Rain, I will not give up. Failure is only when we quit trying and believing. We just must figure out what hasn't worked, search for what will, and never lose heart.

"For *sin* shall no longer be your master, because you are not under the law, but under grace" (Romans 6:14).

Dear Heavenly Father,

Help me to listen to the leading of the Holy Spirit through Your Word, through my pastor, through Christian friends, through Christian songs, through any and all things in my world that will reveal to me the way to be consistent with who I am in You.

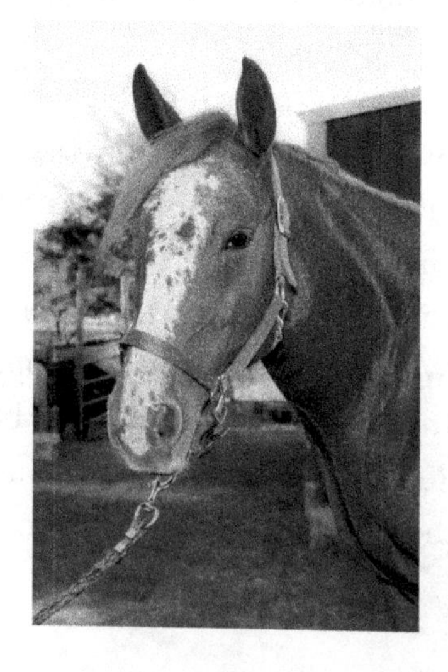

Day 20

T-Thank you, God, that You have led me as a captive in Your ***TRIUMPH*** and that You use me to spread the aroma of the knowledge of You everywhere (2 Corinthians 2:14).

Triumph
(T Verse)

Do you feel that an act of love or kindness is useless unless it changes a situation?

With blossoming lilac bushes comes a fragrance that I have longingly waited for all year. Even though they only last a couple of weeks, they are absolute heaven on earth. I take every opportunity to have a cup of coffee close by and inhale the aroma of the blossoms. What an elaborate gift from God manifested through a simple bush! While the aroma transports moments of elation, its purpose is not to stay, but to bring a temporary reminder of the magnificence of God. Just like us! Yes! God allows us to do similar work through His Spirit. It may be at the grocery store, in a doctor's office, at a restaurant, at church, on a mission trip, at home... God uses us filled with His Spirit to bring reminders of His presence, His power, and His provision. Seldom does His work yield us to long-term relationships, but mere moments to remind those around us that He lives, He loves, and He cares.

"But thanks be to God, who always leads us as captives in Christ's *triumphal* procession and uses us to spread the aroma of the knowledge of Him everywhere" (2 Corinthians 2:14).

Dear God,

Help me to remember that I am the fragrance of Your love to a hurting and lost world around me. Help me be faithful to seize each moment. Help me to not become dismayed because Your work through me does not always fix things, but help me celebrate each moment *triumphantly* that You increase, and I decrease, and You live through me today.

DAY 21

U-Thank you, God, that to those who love you, all things work together ***UNTO*** good (Roman 8:28).

Lay Where You are Located (U Verse)

Does everything have to be going just right for God to work through your life, or are you available when you are tired, weary, and your prayers have not been answered?

Have you ever heard the saying, *"Bloom where you are planted"*? Well, today there was definitely a new perspective on that saying. After a hurried day, we accidentally left the feed sack in the chicken coop. Amazingly, we found a surprise the next morning in that feed sack, a chicken! As if that wasn't enough, upon taking the chicken out, we found an egg! The chicken laid an egg while in that horrible sack overnight! She did what she was created to do regardless of what was going on in her world.

With all of that happening, I had to ask myself, "What about me?" How faithful am I to be available to God when things are difficult, as well as when things are good? How faithful am I when fatigue, depression, anxiety, sickness, death, poverty, conflict, or betrayal enter my world? Do I lay my egg when I'm in a sack? Philippians 4:11 tells us to be content in whatever circumstances that we are in. It is during these times that others notice a difference in me and are drawn to what it is that makes that difference. It is during these times that I can share life and life abundantly. If through my pain and tribulation, I can share hope with another; then there is a purpose in that pain that exceeds my discomfort.

"And we know that in all things God works for the good of those who love him" (Romans 8:28).

Dear Heavenly Father,

Help me when the circumstances of my life get difficult to stay faithful to my calling and my purpose. Help me to share salvation and Your love with those who are hurting through Christ.

Day 22

V-Thank you, God, that I have this treasure in earthen ***VESSEL*** that the excellency of the power is of God and not me (2 Corinthians 4:7).

Moment of Truth
(V Verse)

Are you compliant with Christ's request or submissive? Do you believe that there is a moment of truth for Christians? Do you serve Christ when it is convenient?

Like her name, Sapphire, the mini foal this year is as beautiful as a polished stone. Her antics just make her more adorable. In a dead run, she loves to make circles in the paddock. She is a burst of energy. She loves to be petted, scratched, and snuggled with upon her approval. She is an absolute delight. She seems to follow obediently around the yard and respond to the beckoning to leave things and areas alone that are off limits. However, there is something in horse training that is called the *moment of truth.* This is when a horse is asked to do what they do not want to do. Horses have a nature to please if they have been raised around you, so compliance is sometimes present without submission. I deliberately will ask a young horse to do what I know they will not want to do to establish submission at an early age.

My mother can give testimony of the need to establish this submission when the stature is small as she walked out of the front door and observed me holding Sapphire around the stomach while I was lying flat on my back. We were having a *moment of truth*. She wanted to go, and I wanted her to stay. She proceeded to buck, kick, and rear to get away. She absolutely cannot get away with it because she will be twice as bad the next time, so I must hold her any way that I can. Fortunately, we only must go through this a few times and then remind her occasionally.

I cannot help but shake my head in disbelief when I think of the nature of rebellion. Be it a horse or me, we do not like to be told that we cannot do what we want to do. Upon the moment of salvation, I turned away from that nature of sin as God made me a new creation in Him. Even in turning away, it is still part of my existence until I am perfect with my Savior. I call it a shadow. It is not who I am, but it is present. I'm so glad that my excellence is in God, not me, while I am sojourning in life. I can experience and fellowship with God because it's not me, it's Him!

"But we have this treasure in earthen *vessels,* that the excellency of the power may be of God, and not of us" (2 Corinthians 4:7, KJV).

Dear Heavenly Father,

Help me to live in the excellence that Your Son paid for with His precious life. You would never have given Your Son if there was any way that I could achieve it on my own. I'm so thankful for the joy, peace, and love that envelope my life all because of Your excellence.

Day 23

W-Thank You, God, that when I pass through the ***WATERS***, You will be with me and through the rivers, they shall not overflow me, and when I walk through the fire, I shall not be burned, neither shall the flames kindle upon me. (Isaiah 43:2).

A Lift
(W Verse)

Do you have time set aside to just be in God's presence? Do you feel that you have to be busy all the time to be serving God?

Being gone for a few days, we left our little New Life Trails turtle, Tiny Tim, with my daughter. Tiny Tim has an aquarium with gravel and rocks for his habitat. I thought he had all he needed. However, when we returned to pick him up, my daughter had put a ceramic pineapple in his aquarium for him to climb out of the water, rest, and absorb the sun. I never thought about him needing to get out of the water. He is a water turtle!

In reflection, I couldn't help but think of my daily walk with God. Each day, I am so busy with the details of life, even my service to God. I think I am fine. (swimming around in the aquarium). I must ask myself, "Am I really?" What about that quiet time where I bask in His presence in praise and worship when I am filling up on the things that are true, noble, right, pure, lovable, and excellent after the world has drained me with its darkness.

"When thou passest through the *waters*, I *will be* with thee; and through the rivers, they shall not overflow thee: when thou walkest through the fire, thou shalt not be burned; neither shall the flame kindle upon thee" (Isaiah 43:2, KJV).

Dear Heavenly Father,

Help me to be sure that I have the resources like praise music, special sermons, devotion books, or anything that You can use as a *lift* to keep the waters from overflowing me and the fire burning me in this violent raging world.

DAY 24

X- Thank you, God, that though I am troubled on every side, yet I'm not distressed, ***PERPLEXED***, but not in despair; persecuted, but not forsaken; cast down, but not destroyed; always bearing about in the body the dying of the Lord Jesus, that the life also of Jesus might be made manifest in my mortal flesh (2 Corinthians 4:8–9).

Afterwards
(X Verse)

Have you ever felt like God is unfeeling, and standing back watching you experience the heartbreaking difficulties of life? Do you see Him as disconnected and separate from the knife stabbing pain of life?

I do know that we all have different perspectives on so many things in life. However, as I perceive Scripture, I do not see God as detached and separate from pain. In Hebrews 4:15, the Word tells us that we do not have a high priest who is unable to sympathize, but in every way, He has experienced what we experience but without despair (sin). I believe that despair in itself is not sin unless you turn to the world to alleviate it. When Jesus hung on the cross, he bore the sin of the world. He felt every needle of the drug users, every rape, every sexual abuse, every strike of abuse upon the innocent, every starving child, and so forth. He felt everything. He was there and experienced it with us. I believe, as a believer, that the Holy Spirit lives within me and feels everything. In Ephesians 4:30, God's Word instructs us to not grieve the Holy Spirit. Grieving is not just watching; He is with me, feeling the agony as I scream for escape from the darkest, emptiest nights that will not end.

When we started New Life Trails, we had 3 horses, and only one of them was rideable by the students. Today, we have ten horses that are ridden. When I watch them on the Trail as they ride, I am amazed at the work that God has done to bring New Life Trails where it is today. Some of the hardest work has been helping students understand the guidelines. At times, I have felt hopeless. From keeping the tack as it must be cared for, to how the horse must be saddled and bridled, to when, where, and how the horse is to be rode, to finalizing their time with the horse and making sure they are fed, watered, stall mucked, and everything put up is a challenge. Let's not even talk about teaching them to all get along! Anyway, as much as it is a blessing, it has been difficult and overwhelming at times.

It's not hard to correlate the challenges at the Trails with the challenges of my spiritual life. There are so many different feelings, struggles, and pains. Attempting to process them all and find some kind of rationale is one of my greatest challenges. Not only the events that transpire in my own life, but in so many lives that surround me. There is truly so much neglect and abuse that it can be despairing at times. At the end of the day, **afterwards**, it all comes back to faith and alternatives. I may not always like the path that I must walk with God, but what is the alternative? I've heard it said that the worst day with God is better than the best day without Him. I would agree.

> We are troubled on every side, yet not distressed; we are *perplexed*, but not in despair; Persecuted, but not forsaken; cast down, but not destroyed; Always bearing about in the body the dying of the Lord Jesus, that the life also of Jesus might be made manifest in our body. For we which live are always delivered unto death for

Jesus' sake, that the life also of Jesus might be made manifest in our mortal flesh.

2 Corinthians 4:8-11, KJV

Dear Heavenly Father,

Help me remember that You are Emmanuel, God with us. You are with me through every heartache. Help me remember that if the eye had no tear, the soul would have no rainbow **afterwards**.

DAY 25

Y-Thank you God, that I can come to You and find rest when I am burdened and weary, and I can take Your ***YOKE*** upon me and learn from You for You are gentle and humble and I can find rest for my soul" (Matthew 11:28–29).

Whittling
(Y Verse)

Do you ask God before you take on new projects or commitments?

Even though New Life Trails is all about the outdoors and animals, there is a huge stack of paperwork involved. Working hard on a stack of that paperwork, the lead in my pencil broke. I'm an old timer, so I grew up where I used a knife to sharpen a pencil. For an abundance of reasons, I had a knife on my desk. I quickly grabbed the knife and started whittling away. When I was about finished, I looked up and the pencil sharpener caught my eye. "Hmmmm?" I thought and concluded that I must enjoy doing things the hard way. Unfortunately, that is not just a situation with whittling pencils.

In the Old Testament, there were 613 laws that had to be kept to be right with God. It was impossible for an individual to even think about keeping all the law, yet they tried day after day. This load that they carried each day was synonymous with the heavy yoke that an ox wore around its neck to pull a cart. However, in the New Testament, Jesus paid the price of the law and carried that load for us. The Bible says in Romans 8:1, "So in Christ, our sins have been forgiven and there is no condemnation." We only have to admit that we are lost without Him, believe in who He is, and confess our commitment (repent, turn away from sin) to Him and we are right with God. That is not only for salvation (life), but for the abundant life of daily being with Him despite our inadequacies. Can you feel it…? Like the wind gently brushing against your cheek…freedom…joy, peace, love…so free. "If the Son has set you free, you are free indeed" (John 8:36).

"Come unto Me all who are weary and heavy burdened and I will give you rest. Take my *yoke* upon you, and learn from me; for I am gentle and humble and you will find rest for your souls" (Matthew 11:28–29).

Dear Heavenly Father,

Help me to remember the tremendous price that You paid for my spiritual freedom. Help me live that freedom to the fullest and share it with all those that come into my world. Help me continually to be mindful that this life is not about doing, but being. It's about walking, talking, loving, and sharing this life that You gave us with You.

Day 26

Z-Thank you, God, that if the Son shall make me ***FREE***,
I am free indeed (John 8:36).

Crossing Over
(Z Verse)

Do you often think of the price or the privilege of freedom? Have you had a time in your life that you accessed that freedom and crossed over?

Filling the Trails with laughter and delight, twenty children relished God's creation on a beautiful day filled with rays of sunshine and gentle life-giving breezes. They scampered through trees, jumped the creeks, journeyed through the terrain, all while enjoying the living creatures that God created. As I watched and listened, I thought of freedom. Regardless of where they came from, or what circumstances encapsulated their lives, for this moment, they seemed so *free*. Surrounded by the Bible verses engraved upon wood on trees, and a God that desired to engrave them onto their hearts consistent with His plans, His provisions, His promises, and His love, they seemed so free.

As Dahli, our llama, met the children while playing on the bridge, they came to a screeching halt. Dahli 's elegant way of maneuvering himself with contemplation and evaluation as he observed the children made me think of a verse of scripture, John 5:24. In this verse, we are exhorted that if we believe and accept that salvation comes through Jesus as our Savior, we have *CROSSED OVER* from death to life. As I watched the children,

I knew each one of them would come to a time in their lives that they would accept or reject Jesus as their Savior. At that point, they would cross over the bridge from eternal death to eternal life, just as they desired to cross over the bridge that Dahli was so gracefully guarding.

Thank you, God, that if the Son shall make me free, I am free indeed (John 8:36).

Dear Heavenly Father,

Your Son paid such a high price for freedom. Help me to always be mindful, thankful, and willing to share that freedom with all.

Day 27

"As *iron* sharpens *iron*, so one person sharpens another" (Proverbs 27:17).

Iron

As I shuffled through the leaves into the clearing that homed Sunflower and Jack, two of New Life Trail's goats, I observed them playing. Sunflower is expecting kids at any time, and she is heavily laden with them. In addition, she is our little milking goat. Each morning, her udders are filled to the maximum! So, you can understand why I was surprised to see her frolicking with Jack through the pasture. She was running, jumping, and kicking up her heels, or hoofs, should I say. Jack was leading and bursting with energy as he is young, lightweight, and full of energy. Jack's behavior didn't surprise me, but Sunflower's did. She usually walks slowly and sits most of the day chewing her cud. However, being in the presence of Jack had lifted her spirits, lightened her heart, and gave her energy and strength that she had not tapped into and practiced for some time.

Correspondingly, is it not the same way with us as believers? How many times do we find ourselves heavily laden with the responsibilities and cares of fulfilling our duties as a believer? We simply seem content to contemplate, sit, and sedentarily chew on the Word of God. Then miraculously, a new believer who is excited and invigorated in the new life in Christ is jumping and skipping around and sharing Jesus' hope, love, and life. Then, suddenly, we find ourselves with a new and fresh excitement about life and the abundant life in God that Jesus bought for us with His precious blood.

Dear Heavenly Father,

Help me to look for where You are working and join You there with others in anticipation and excitement. I can see you gazing upon us and a smile adorning Your face as You watch Your children filled with excitement, sharing, loving, and living in You.

Day 28

"There is a way which seemeth right unto a man, but the end thereof are the ways of death" (Proverbs 14:12, KJV).

Further than You Want to Go

Wanting to help at the Trails, I asked a couple of volunteers to go to the back of the pasture to check the fence, as we were going to let the animals graze it because of the severe shortage of hay. Interestingly, it was just a short time before they were back at the office with a troubled demeanor. They proclaimed that the truck was stuck in the mud. We are in a drought, so that left me bewildered for a second. Then, they explained that they were going to take a shortcut through the pond, which was dried up. My eyebrows raised and instantly I knew what had happened. The pond dries hard on top, but underneath the top layer there are feet of soggy soil. Appearances can be very deceiving!

Likewise, many times in my life, I've wanted to take a shortcut when there wasn't a shortcut to be taken. Yes, the situation had an appearance of being the solution, but in reality, the answer led to sin. A definition of sin is missing the mark. When sin is present, it will take you further than you want to go and keep you longer than you want to stay, just like the old pickup that is still in the pond waiting for the ground to dry around it enough to pull it out.

Dear Heavenly Father,

Forgive me for the nature that I have—to take the seemingly easy way, but end up in so much more trouble. Whether I'm trying to lose weight fast, make quick money, halfway do a job, bypass the healing process of pain, settle for a relationship, or jump ahead of Your answer, help me to always be aware. Help me to be aware that Satan is like a roaring lion seeking to devour me and he comes to kill, steal, and destroy. He WILL take me further than I want to go and keep me longer than I want to stay in trouble.

DAY 29

God's message to Gideon: "And the angel of the LORD appeared unto him, and said unto him, The LORD *is* with thee, thou mighty man of *valour*" (Judges 6:12, KJV).

Valor?

After a wild dog jumped our fence and attacked our precious miniature Pygmy goat, Velvet, and killed her and the kid that she carried, we were so frightened that the dog would return. A friend who raises Great Pyrenees dogs donated a two-month-old puppy to us. Pyrenees are guard dogs and will walk the premises all night and keep guard during the day. They are quiet, introverted, devoted, and self-sacrificing dogs. However, when they placed this ball of fluff in my arms, I just could not see it. Especially after spending time with her and watching her melt every time we picked her up, roll around at the bottom of our feet, and run horrified from the sprinkler. In spite of what we saw at the time, we were told emphatically that inside her was an uncompromising guard dog.

In watching Athena, our Great Pyrenees pup, I couldn't help but think of the story of Gideon in the Bible. Israel was in a desperate state, and they needed a rescuer. "And the angel of the LORD appeared unto him, and said unto him, The LORD *is* with thee, thou mighty man of *valour*" (Judges 6:12, KJV). In spite of Gideon's seeming weaknesses, there truly was a man of *valor* within him in God, just as I know Athena will grow to guard and protect the animals of New Life Trails.

Dear Heavenly Father,

Whether I am looking at myself or others, help me to remember there is more than what can be seen from one moment to the next. Help me to believe in those things that can't always be seen, especially God's promises for my life.

Day 30

"Avoid it, pass not by it, turn from it, and pass away
(Proverbs 4:15, KJV).

Do not Pass by It

As the Bermuda grass peaks from its brown, dark, winter blanket, it can be a blessing and a curse. The first roots of the Bermuda are rich in nutrients and to most animals this is a blessing after a long sparse winter of old dry hay. However, to some animals such as mini horses, it is an enemy of the most deceiving kind. They crave it and are starving for it, but it can founder them. Their bodies are not built to process its richness. As I move the mini horses to dry lots during this time and continue them on hay, it seems wrong. However, I know it is necessary because they do not have the ability to discern what is good and bad for them.

What a similar analogy for our children! Communication, social interaction, immediate contact, peer equality, appeasement, babysitter, academic opportunities—all of these are reasons that I allow technological devices in the hands of my children or even myself. The time seems right, the availability is there, and it looks beyond desirable, but if the timing is wrong, just like the new Bermuda grass, it can be crippling for life. It takes a lot of effort and expense to keep eleven therapy miniature horses off Bermuda. If I want their purpose to come to fruition, *I MUST* stop everything in my world and be attentive.

Dear Heavenly Father,

Help me to be attentive and aggressive in the physical and spiritual aspects of my life with those who are under my watch. Help me to see and know those things that look good but can reap disability in the purpose and plan of lives that you have placed in my story. Help me to examine my own life daily to be sure that I am not into something that can harm me.

DAY 31

"For in the day of trouble, He will keep me safe in His dwelling; He will hide me in the *shelter* of His sacred tent" (Psalm 27:5).

Shelter

Frantic to provide protection for our little mini horses from the hail and strong winds, I proceeded to drive t-posts that would stabilize the corners of an old tarp. After about an hour of work, I felt the rain begin to be released from the heavens that held it captive. Sitting on a stump under a limb, I wanted to watch the mini horses take shelter. I thought they would immediately take haven, but only two sought shelter. Determined to see all my work validated, I continued to watch, even while I became saturated! Dismayed, I hung my head and turkeyed off to the house. (My mom calls walking "turkeyed.") I couldn't help but think of how God has provided *shelter* for us from the storms of life in His Word and work. It wasn't merely an hour of work that God put into preparing our *shelter,* but His very existence and being.

As God gazes down upon the ones that He loves so dearly and sees them disregarding His provision and facing the storms alone, I think dismay is an appropriate expression, but encompasses so much more than I can even imagine with my little ponies.

Dear Heavenly Father,

Help me to be mindful to run to the shelter that You have sacrificially provided for me in Your Word. Help me to memorize your promises until they are not what I know, but who I am.

AFTERWORD

New Life Trails Ministry Association's Mission Statement: *Partnering with animals to get the hearts of individuals to be able to intervene academically, emotionally, socially, and spiritually.*

At this point, you know a lot more about New Life Trails than you originally knew about it. However, you may have more questions than answers about some of the details of the journey. Why do I feel it is important that you know the details of New Life Trail's journey? "*That which we know, we will love.*" This was a quote from my history teacher in college when he was asked *why it is important to know history.*

Volume one of *Enduring Pain, Finding Purpose, Experiencing Peace* is just the beginning of a journey that I want to take with you into the lives of the animals and their experiences at New Life Trails with spiritual analogies. My heart is that as you know our animals, you know their stories, and you know the stories that God has written from interaction with them, that you will love them, and you will love the work that God does through them. Furthermore, we want you to journey with us and the animals as we love the broken-hearted, share salvation with the lost, provide discipleship to the young in Christ, and are the hands, feet, and heart of Jesus through the animals to a lost and hurting world.

To begin with, it was almost twelve years ago, as I was riding our horse Damien through a neighborhood in our town, that I noticed how children just flocked to him to pet and love him. It was at this time that God put into my heart that horses were a tremendous venue to reach individuals with the love of Jesus, *partnering with animals to get the hearts of individuals spiritually.* Later, as I was teaching at a school, I had two students that I was having behavior problems with, and it was interfering with their academics. I could not find a solution. Praying and asking God to show me what to do, He put into my heart to take the students to our pasture and work with them alongside of our three horses, Damien, Windstar, and Lightning. This was the beginning of partnering with the animals to get the children's hearts, *so that I could work with them academically.* It worked! Every day in class, they would ask me about the horses, hug me, and give everything academically.

Subsequently, I will never forget one of my third-grade students sitting on her horse and raising her arms in the air and proclaiming that she could do all things through Christ who strengthened her. When she first came to meet the horses, she was so scared. Each time she came afterward, her fears would subside. It took three times of just sitting on her horse for her to be comfortable enough to move. Now she participates in rodeos and other equine activities. She was an example of our mission statement: *partnering with animals to get the hearts of individuals to intervene socially.*

At this point in time, God used a chosen group of kids, some of them mine, to establish the spiritual component of the Trails. They would come, saddle the horses at sunrise, have a devotional time, and take off riding in the pasture on some trail. We thought *New Life Trails* would be a good name for our special place set aside by God to learn more about Him based on 2 Corinthians 5:17. I wrote it on an old piece of wood that was nearby and nailed it to a stump by an old gate that was our opening to the Trails. In addition, we wrote on individual pieces of wood twenty-six of God's promises, from A to Z. We had put together and used these verses at a Christian school that I worked at for six years. However,

I wanted all students and people to know who they are in Jesus. If they walked the Trail and read them, then they would be refreshed in God or maybe even come to Him for the first time: *partnering with animals to get the hearts of individuals to intervene spiritually.*

Almost a year later, my spiritual and academic partner in this journey and I were asked to run a math camp for two weeks that would focus on at-risk students who had completed third grade. In trying to figure out how to get the students to come every day, God put into my heart to use the horses. However, we had two weeks of camp, and we knew the horses would not keep their attention. So, we decided to bring more animals into the camp even though we had to borrow them. Each day, we chose not to disclose the animals' identities for the next day to entice them to be in attendance. Initially, we brought three fainting goats, a snapping turtle, sheered a sheep, hand painted a white mini horse, and many more. Unfortunately, it was extremely difficult to use borrowed animals that we had not previously worked with or trained. So, this is where the next chapter of the journey began, adding all the other New Life Trails animals to our family. While it began for academic reasons, these animals became a ministry to countless individuals *emotionally, socially, and spiritually*.

A good question at this point is, "Where did we put these animals?" In addition to that question, there was another interesting situation. My husband, being a realist, had told me when our children were younger, and I wanted a farm where we pastured the horses, "We don't live on a farm, and we aren't going to have a farm." Honoring my precious husband that God gave me to watch over, protect, and gently guide me is a critical aspect of this journey. Emphatically, I do not believe that God would have chosen to work through me if I harbored bitterness or strife in my heart at any point as He worked to establish the ministry at

New Life Trails. With that said, after the first year of borrowing the animals, he agreed that we just needed to get our own animals for the camp and continue to work with the students.

Amazingly, God brought the animals to New Life Trails through rescues and donations. The first animals that we received were fainting goats. Having never raised goats, I thought that we could just turn them in with the horses. I was wrong! They instantly ran out of the pasture through our rusted,

dilapidated barbed wire fence. Chasing and screaming at them, we hoped that they would faint as their title indicated, but they did not!

Upon catching them, my husband built a small pen for them from loose wire laying around. Feeling sorry for them being in such a small pen, I started gathering donated pallets from business owners around town. Unfortunately, at this time in our lives, we did not even have money for a fence, nor the wire to attach the pallets together. We gathered loose wire from bales of hay around the pasture. As more animals came to us, we enlarged the area and used the pallets to define the perimeter of their new space. By the time we finished, we had collected over two thousand pallets to build fences and make shelters for the animals. Amazingly, this worked for two years until the pallets became compromised due to being out in the elements.

Wilbur, our first pig, was the main culprit in discovering the pallet's weakening state. Determined, he made his way through the pallets and left the land every evening to visit a nearby trailer park where there was a chestnut tree. I always teased that Wilbur was our first missionary from New Life Trails. As he made his daily ventures and went into all the world, I was going to attach a gospel tract on a collar for him. Most of the residents loved to see him each day as he would come and go, but there was an individual that did not and reported him to the authorities. The next escapee was a sheep that ate the neighbors' flowers, next was a calf, and then... You can see the pattern.

After animal control came and picked up their first escapee, I was quickly at an impasse with no funds for such criminal activity. Not having the money to get him out of jail, God sent two angels into our lives through one of the students that attended a math camp. Desperate, I called this family, and they brought the money to bond the first fugitive out of jail. As God brought them that day, he has continued to use them as we have built fences, shelters, pens, rescued horses, pigs, and everything else that can be imagined. Only heaven could reward their selfless labor for years to New Life Trails. However, being frustrated at this point and not knowing what direction financially God wanted us to go, I petitioned Him with great fervor to show me some direction. I wanted the animals to bring peace and Jesus' love, not trouble.

Within only a few days, our pastor called and asked if our church could come out to the land to help build a new fence and anything else that we needed on a day called *The Great Day of Service.* We had 250 people take down the pallets, burn them and put up a good fence, cut sticker trees, clear brush, and help build structures for the animals. It was truly a miracle of God watching all those people working like ants out there while wearing their neon yellow *Great Day of Service* t-shirts.

After spending that time with the animals, individuals at church would continually ask me how the animals were doing. It was from these inquiries that I asked our pastor if I could share updates on the animals on our church prayer chain. After only a few times, the updates became stories about the animals with spiritual analogies. I wanted to give back to everyone through the stories for all the prayers, support, and financial help that my church and others breathed into New Life Trails. I have written 315 stories to this date, and this devotion book is the beginning of sharing the previous and future stories that God speaks into my heart.

After the *Great Day of Service*, God opened the door to the many needs of New Life Trails. There have been so many that He has chosen and anointed to prepare for the ministry at the Trails. Beyond my understanding, he led a man to develop and guide the construction of two bridges, a rock trail, and our precious Logan's Barn. As well as many others to build the office, install electricity, build the hay barn, and the list goes on and on. Why do I take the time to mention all the details of the journey for New Life Trails? Remember*, that which we know, we love.* Not only do we love, but we understand what a great love that our Heavenly Father has for us to go to the length to write this love letter to you using his creation and on old simple country girl that loves her Heavenly Father and the creation that He made for her.

Today, New Life Trails has become an integral part of the community as we work with hospice, nursing homes, schools, churches, boys and girls clubs, Big Brother and Big Sister programs, youth shelters, autistic foundation, disabled veteran groups, mentoring, tutoring, horse therapy, birthday parties, social gatherings, and any other work that God wants to use his magnificent creations for: *to get the hearts of individuals to be able to intervene academically, socially, emotionally, and spiritually.*

About the Author

Living on the edge of Ponca City for thirty years, God has allowed me to continue to enjoy and share the world that I grew up in through New Life Trails. While I've lived many places growing up, home was my Grandma Bell's farm near Skedee, Oklahoma. I trekked the pastures, creeks, and farmland with my three older brothers and two younger sisters. Being enamored with God through His creation, I gave my heart to Him in a blanket of green pasture with a gentle breeze whispering upon my cheeks and the warmth of the sun caressing my face when I was ten.

Currently, I am a special education teacher living with my husband of thirty years after raising our four children. God has allowed many tools of ministry to be part of my story, from poverty, suicide, abandonment, many different kinds of abuse, depression, divorce, rejection, children's home, foster care, the falling away of a child, and many more pearls that have been ground in the friction of a clam. These incidents do not define me; they equip me to work with all types of brokenness in individuals who do not know of salvation or of the abundant life Jesus gave His life for.

The purpose of New Life Trails is to provide a place that you may find life and life abundantly through Jesus our Savior and His Word (John 10:10). We believe that when you find a purpose for your life in Jesus, then you will coincidingly find a purpose for the pain that life has left on your doorstep. In that purpose, you will find peace.

It encompasses an area that contains three crosses, the plan of salvation on wood, and even a prayer to guide you.

The Trails are lined with twenty-six pieces of wood attached to trees that contain a Bible verse memory plan, so that your family can begin to hide God's Word in your hearts (Psalm 119:11).

Those verses, and even a calendar with the verses, are available at newlifetrails.org.

CPSIA information can be obtained
at www.ICGtesting.com
Printed in the USA
BVHW052004210323
660860BV00004B/11